# Between Two F...

**Sylvia Pankhurst**

## Arranged and edited by Rachel Holmes

*methuen* | drama

LONDON · NEW YORK · OXFORD · NEW DELHI · SYDNEY

METHUEN DRAMA
Bloomsbury Publishing Plc
50 Bedford Square, London, WC1B 3DP, UK
1385 Broadway, New York, NY 10018, USA
29 Earlsfort Terrace, Dublin 2, Ireland

BLOOMSBURY, METHUEN DRAMA and the Methuen
Drama logo are trademarks of Bloomsbury Publishing Plc

First published in Great Britain 2022

Cover design by Jade Barnett

Cover image: Sylvia Pankhurst by Sylvia Pankhurst
© National Portrait Gallery, London

A catalogue record for this book is available from the British Library.

A catalog record for this book is available from the Library of Congress.

ISBN: PB: 978-1-3503-5384-8
ePDF: 978-1-3503-5385-5
eBook: 978-1-3503-5386-2

Series: Modern Plays

Typeset by Mark Heslington Ltd, Scarborough, North Yorkshire
Printed and bound in Great Britain

To find out more about our authors and books visit
www.bloomsbury.com and sign up for our newsletters.

# Introduction, by Helen Pankhurst

Acts of resistance take different forms. My grandmother, Sylvia Pankhurst, was an authority on most – all her life, wearing her causes on her sleeve. Approaches and tactics included: pamphleteering; petitioning; demonstrating; editing and writing of letters, articles and books; decorating halls with imagery and colour on buildings; making billboards and banners and holding them up in marches; objects in homes; badges, sashes, clothes, jewellery . . . with a bit of lateral thinking almost everything could be used to raise awareness and call for change.

Since Sylvia's first form of defiance was as a suffragette, she was also engaged in militancy, including stone throwing and using her own body – her life – as physical resistance. The hunger-striking in prison resulting in the horrors of being force-fed. When she was first incarcerated in 1906, aged only twenty-four, Sylvia fought back in different ways. Some of her sketches were used to show what life was like and her description of the experience of being force-fed was widely shared, including among the mainstream media. They remain some of the most moving and powerful testimonies of the torture inflicted by the state on the suffragettes.

When imprisoned in 1920/21 for sedition because of her socialist campaigning, Sylvia also wrote poetry as a way of passing the time, a way of reflecting and continuing to resist. She then published the poems as a collection called *Writ on Cold Slate*. The title of the collection comes from the poem below.

## Writ on Cold Slate

Whilst many a poet to his love hath writ,
boasting that thus he gave immortal life,
my faithful lines upon inconstant slate,
destined to swift execution reach not thee.

In other ages dungeons might be strange,
with ancient mouldiness their airs infect,

but kindly warders would the tablets bring,
so captives might their precious thoughts inscribing,
the treasures of the fruitful mind preserve,
and culling thus its flowers, postpone decay.

Only this age that loudly boasts Reform,
hath set its seal of vengeance 'gainst the mind,
decreeing thought in prison shall be writ,
save on cold slate and swiftly washed away.

The difficulty of expressing herself in prison when it
was so hard to get access to paper and pencil cannot be
underestimated, the poem above speaks to that. It is
therefore particularly poignant that some of what Sylvia did
manage to write and smuggle out, and which my father
deposited at the British Library, is only now coming to light
in the *Toilet Paper Transcripts* that Rachel Holmes has
meticulously put together.

And they are astonishing in many ways.

Firstly, it's a script for a play. How could Sylvia even conceive
of such a feat when she only had standard-issue prison toilet
paper and a pencil to hand? How did she do so, when she
couldn't keep notes, couldn't spread out her papers, when
even going over to edit individual words or sentences was
difficult and could pierce the toilet roll?

Secondly, Sylvia had by this stage written in many different
forms . . . but as far as we know, had not attempted to write
something as ambitious as a play, so why now? Why this form
and this large an undertaking? One can only assume that she
wanted something to keep her mind occupied for longer
during the six-month imprisonment period, leaving behind
the grim realities of prison for much longer than was possible
during the writing of a short poem. The writing of a play was a
way to relive, to conjure up the past and some specific people,
and maybe particularly past choices and past conversations.

And this links to the content of the script. It focuses on the
political and personal lives of Noah Adamson, clearly a

pseudonym for Keir Hardie, and it includes the character of Freda – obviously, Sylvia herself. It speaks to the experiences of poverty, pay gaps, poor working and living conditions and how politicians such as Keir Hardie and those around him – including female community activists – tried to do something in practical and strategic ways and the obstacles and vested interests they encountered. As usual for Sylvia, the addressing of envelopes and the folding of circulars, i.e. the hands-on realities of politicking and of people's lives are given attention – not taken for granted.

What we also have is the uneasy relationship between feminism and left-wing politics, including specifically between the Women's Social and Political Union, WSPU, and the Independent Labour Party, ILP. The play shows how Keir Hardie tried to support the cause for women getting the vote despite the unpopularity within his party of this position. Likewise, the fact that the suffragette leadership increasingly distanced themselves from the ILP.

By the time Sylvia was writing, Keir Hardie had been dead for seven years, one can only assume there were aspects of the man or of their relationship that Sylvia wanted to explore, relive and possibly even share. I also expect it was the concerns around their relationship, or the way the personal and political intertwined and her own anxiety about not doing anything that would hurt others, including Keir Hardie's political career, that she wanted to reflect on and put to paper.

Unfortunately, the play was not completed or parts of the script were lost. However, I'm delighted that in the pages that follow, we can get a glimpse of the world she created or recreated to escape her physical incarceration. The fact that she kept the precious realms of toilet paper also suggest that the personal and political content continued to matter to her. She didn't want them extinguished – with this publication, they have come to light.

# Between Two Fires

An unpublished three-act play by Sylvia Pankhurst written in Holloway prison in 1921

Arranged and edited by Rachel Holmes

The Toilet Paper Transcripts

SYLVIA PANKHURST, HOLLOWAY 1921

## Rachel Holmes Transcripts – BL M/S collections

Original manuscript: written in soft pencil on pieces of standard-issue HM Prison toilet paper, 5x4 inches, most perforated into individual pieces, otherwise in strips of 2/3 pieces unperforated, unsorted and jumbled up in several A4 brown buff envelopes, unopened since Richard Pankhurst donated them to the British Library. Prohibited writing materials other than a slate and chalk for most of her sentence, Sylvia improvised.

Some of the pieces of toilet paper manuscript are numbered, others not. There are from three to seven successive drafts of each scene, section and fragment of the play, with duplicate page numbers rarely corresponding to previous drafts. Scenes, sections and fragments are frequently erased and overwritten, the original pencil indent still visible, but illegible. Where there are legible strikethroughs, I have been able to retain the original.

The hundreds of pages of manuscript are randomly interleaved with letters, poems, speeches and organisational notes, sometimes enjambed on the same piece of toilet paper.

The sections of manuscript and correspondence were smuggled out of Holloway in small bundles by released prisoners and Sylvia's nominated visitors, usually Norah Smyth. Some sections never made it, went missing, or perhaps were never written beyond draft notes. Remaining true to Sylvia's scene order, the play structure presented here is therefore a necessarily partial reconstruction from the surviving parts of the manuscript that were successfully saved and retrieved by these clandestine means: Act I, scenes 1–3 and Act 3, scenes 1 and 4. I sorted and transcribed the manuscript over a period of seven months in the British Library Manuscripts Reading Room.

## BETWEEN TWO FIRES

This title is my own, since the surviving manuscript is untitled and I have yet to find one suggested in Sylvia's archives. The phrase is spoken in the play by Freda McLaird – the Sylvia figure – to Noah Adamson – Keir Hardie – and to me expresses the entwined themes of the piece: the political story of the relationship between the Labour Party and the women's movement, and the personal relationship between Sylvia and Keir Hardie and their families. Sylvia explores how the British socialist and feminist movements evolved together and why they diverged, documenting from her first hand, insider's experience how the Labour Party tried to come to terms with the suffragette campaign for Votes for Women and, particularly, the Women's Social and Political Union, WSPU, led by Sylvia's mother Emmeline and her elder sister Christabel.

The title phrase, spoken by Sylvia/Freda, equally expresses Keir Hardie/Noah's dilemma in finding himself caught between the two fires of his wife and mother of his children, Lillie, and his lover and soulmate, Sylvia.

**Freda**  You're between two fires.

**Noah**  They're very warm sometimes.

Sylvia Pankhurst, dramatising her own story, makes this explicit in the scene in which this exchange appears, where Noah asks Freda to draw close and come and sit by the fire where they discuss their love. Sylvia's own response to the struggle of loving an elder, married man is deeply inscribed in the later surviving sections of the play, in the most broken-off, erased and then overwritten fragments, mostly indecipherable, all written clandestinely in solitary confinement five years after Hardie's death.

Underlining in the text below is all Sylvia's.

**Characters** *(in order of appearance)*

*Cast of 26 characters: 13 female, 13 male*

| | |
|---|---|
| Ruth Glasier | a brisk young woman about twenty-five, a clerk giving her evenings to campaigning |
| Nellie Monday | a factory worker aged eighteen with fair hair and pink cheeks, community activist, later a young married woman about thirty |
| Winnie | a bright girl of fourteen, community activist |
| Jack | Winnie's brother, also a volunteer |
| Peter Jane | an old man of seventy, community activist |
| Mrs – | a pale little woman washing teacups and tidying |
| Old Woman | in a black shawl, clean white apron and chenille hairnet, her hands thin and trembling |
| Tom Fenton | between forty-five & fifty years of age with grey hair cut short. Clean-shaven wearing spectacles, of medium height and rather spare, neatly dressed in quiet grey clothes and might be anything in the world from a clerk to a bank manager |
| Hugh Pratt | about fifty years of age, a slight man in dark well-worn clothes |
| Noah Adamson | white haired and a little stouter than Hugh Pratt, not yet fifty, but at first sight appears much older |
| Kate Conway | socialist-feminist bluestocking, an Independent Labour Party founder, she has achieved a degree in classics at Newnham College and defies the current practice of Cambridge University refusing to award degrees |

|  |  |
|---|---|
|  | to women by appending BA to her name |
| Mrs Hawkins | working woman, community activist who mothers all the younger women |
| Caroline | young woman who has taken the suffragette pledge of citizenship to fight for votes for women |
| Martin | a Labour activist |
| Donovan | a Labour activist |
| Bill Fermer | a Labour politician |
| Tom Smith | a Labour politician |
| Mrs Bullen | chicken factory worker, trade unionist, feminist, community leader |
| Annie | a Labour activist |
| Dick Pyke | a pale, very ragged boy about sixteen years of age, gas worker, trade unionist |
| Mrs Carter | stout and ruddy, garment worker, seamstress, socialist-feminist, community activist |
| Nellie* | a young woman, new volunteer activist, finding her way *(a different character from Nellie Monday) |
| Freda McLaird | about twenty-five years, socialist-feminist, suffragette, community activist |
| George Barker | a fat short red-faced man with a heavy gold watch chain |
| Mr Dickson | a tall pale man in a frock coat and silk hat rather pale and bored looking |
| Mr Lyle | of medium height with light-grey silk spats and a white waistcoat with a dark black beard, white teeth and a rather bland appearance, air of a merchant-banker, Liberal Party major donor |

*Key to pseudonyms and real names, where indicated by Sylvia Pankhurst in manuscript.*

*For the corresponding life stories and political biographies of the many other recognisable and/or composite historical characters in the play, see my* Sylvia Pankhurst: Natural Born Rebel *(London: Bloomsbury, 2020).*

| | |
|---|---|
| Noah Adamson | Keir Hardie |
| Freda McLaird | Sylvia Pankhurst |
| Kate Conway/Glasier | Socialist-feminist politician and writer, referred to affectionately as the 'grandmother of the British Labour movement'. Born Katharine St John Conway, she married Scottish socialist politician Bruce Glasier. |
| Ruth Glasier | Sister to Bruce Glasier, later Kate Conway's sister-in-law. |
| Hugh Pratt | Frank Smith, socialist politician, founding member of ILP and its first parliamentary candidate, friend, confidant, sometime political secretary to Keir Hardie |

# Act I

## Scene One

### Noah Adamson's committee Rooms in a London Constituency

*An upstairs room with uncarpeted floor trestle tables piled with literature. Walls covered with a drab faded wallpaper torn and discoloured and hung with posters.* **Ruth Glasier** *a brisk young woman about twenty-five, a clerk giving her evenings to the work, is addressing envelopes.* **Nellie Monday** *a factory worker aged eighteen with fair hair and pink cheeks is putting circulars in envelopes.* **Winnie** *a bright girl of fourteen is doing the same.* **Jack** (**Winnie***'s brother*) *is folding circulars.* **Peter Jane** *an old man of seventy is also folding circulars. Mrs – a pale little woman is washing teacups, dusting and tidying. These are all of the working class.*

**Nellie**   Oh I do hope he'll get in! I don't know what I shall do if we lose the election.

**Ruth**   We've all got to make ourselves responsible for seeing that we win! Don't let's have any talk of losing here! Mind you don't leave out the pollings, Winnie, and put them inside the election address if you please!

*Enter an old woman in a black shawl and clean white apron and a chenille hairnet. Her hands are very thin and trembling.*

**Old Woman**   Is Mr Adamson in, Miss?

**Ruth Glasier**   No but I can give him a message.

**Old Woman**   Please Miss. My sister is lying in the infirmary, and she says all the women there are asking for Mr Adamson . . .

---

*[missing section]*

**Scene Two**

*[unnumbered] – Directions: . . .* **Tom Fenton** *between forty-five
and fifty years of age with grey hair cut short. Clean-shaven wearing
spectacles, of medium height and rather spare. Is neatly dressed in
quiet grey clothes and might be anything in the world from a clerk to
a bank manager.*

**Hugh Pratt** *is about fifty years of age, a slight man in dark well-
worn clothes.*

**Noah**'s *hair is white and he is a little stouter. He wears a brown
tweed coat with darker trousers. He is not yet fifty but at first sight
appears much older.*

**Noah Adamson**    Ah, there I agree with you! The
Suffragette question being set aside by the Labour Party in
favour of a direct fight to secure Socialism. My feeling would
be very different, but we are only too aware that the Party
has not got so far as that, and that the majority of the
Parliamentary Party and the Executive are actually afraid of
socialism or even opposed to it. No, Fenton, this is not a
question of Votes for Women or Socialism. The question of
Socialism has to got to be fought <u>inside the Labour Party
unfortunately</u>. And even you, Tom, are keen on pressing for
Reforms – old-age Pensions, unemployment, and education
Bills, palliative measures only indirectly consistent with the
fight for Socialism.

**Tom Fenton**    Oh, don't misunderstand me, Adamson, I'm
<u>not</u> against your helping the women in the least. I only wish
the Party would take up their question and get it settled.
What I mean is, I do not think it worth splitting the Party on
such an issue. Moreover, I don't think you could split the
Party on it. If you were to, you would isolate yourself and
lose your influence, which is so necessary just now. You
would cut yourself off from office in the Party, lose the
Chairmanship and your seat on the Executive and leave the
field clear to the reactionaries.

**Noah**   My influence would not be worth much if I gave way to the reactionaries at every point and allowed them to govern my actions.

**Fenton**   Nobody wants you to do that, Adamson, but if you belong to a democratically governed Party you have got to obey the decisions of the majority even when they go against you. You can't get yourself above them.

**Noah**   That can be carried too far, Fenton. I cannot submit to being present to give my support to a just cause and from standing by those who are making a brave fight under very difficult circumstances.

**Fenton**   If you can arrange matters so as to keep your personal freedom to act as you pleased till the majority is ready to act with you, well and good. But don't be rash, Adamson. Remember what is at stake. And you have given the best years of your life to creating a Labour Party. At present you are recognized as its leader. That gives you an immense advantage in bringing the Party on towards Socialism. It would be a thousand pities to throw away your position in the movements for something that, after all, is not Socialism.

Already your influence has been weakened by your support of the WSPU. You are held to a certain extent responsible for more abnormal actions of theirs. And the WSPU ostentatiously declares it does not support the Labour Party 'any more than any other Party.' Miss Christabel, with her airy insistence on the neutrality of her precious Union, takes the wind out of your sails, in my opinion. In fact, she puts you in a devil of a hole to my mind. Neither you nor anyone can expect the Labour Party, or the Liberals for that matter, to take kindly to such a method! And isn't she impudent, upon my word!

**Noah**   If the Labour Party could have been induced to make the women's question its own the situation would have been entirely different. Even now if one of the places secured by the Labour Members in the Ballot had been given to the Women's Bill, the WSPU's neutral electoral policy would inevitably have been dropped.

**Fenton**  I wish something could have been arranged for the General Election but agents complained bitterly that our most efficient women speakers were not supporting our candidates but were on WSPU platforms declaring neutrality, belittling the Labour Party and stirring people up to go and heckle our candidates. Our best women canvassers were getting themselves thrown out of government candidate's meetings or going on poster parades to advertise Mrs Pankhurst's meetings. On polling day instead of bringing up the voters, they did nothing but waste their energy shouting 'Keep the Liberals out!'

**Noah**  If my policy had been adopted we should have had the women with us.

**Fenton**  But that wasn't your reason for advocating it.

**Noah**  No, I support their demand because it is the right thing to do.

**Fenton**  Well I warn you, Adamson: they'll give you a lot of trouble before you've done with them. No-one is readier than I to admit that Mrs Sedgfield has done splendid work for the ILP in her time and I know that the WSPU was entirely formed of Socialist women in the first place, but they are getting some very odd recruits nowadays. This neutral policy and the fact that they happen to be attacking a <u>Liberal</u> Government appeals to a most reactionary set of women who only want the vote as a barrier to progress and to stop any social legislation.

Socialism has quite a back seat in the WSPU now; indeed there's no blinking the fact that it's out of it altogether. Miss Christabel is a dark horse. I shouldn't be the least surprised at her turning Tory and dragging her mother along with her. They had a queer crowd down with them at Tonford. One good lady complained tearfully in all her speeches that they won't even let us have our catechism in our schools! You can guess that didn't interest a working-class audience much, but they always had a rattling good working woman to follow her. Mrs Sedgefield was driving about with a couple of titled ladies and created quite a sensation amongst the Primrose dames I am told. And yet she keeps her grip on the working women, the Socialist Women too, and the best of them: it's wonderful how she manages it. She is certainly a loss to us. I am with you there. But it is no use crying over spilt milk. The situation is going to be highly complicated. Take my advice Noah and give it a wide berth. Tell them to row their own cause without you.

**Noah**   One can't shuffle off one's responsibility towards public questions so easily as that, Tom.

**Fenton**   Oh, I know what you are with that conscience of yours. And you'll go your own way whatever one says to you. But take care: don't do anything in a hurry. Don't be impatient, take a long view of things and remember we of the ILP are counting on you. (*Taking out his watch.*) Well I shall have to be going I've just about time to get the 4.30.

**Noah**   Goodbye, Tom. I hope you'll be down again soon.

**Fenton**   Goodbye, Adamson. Goodbye, Pratt.

**Hugh Pratt**   Goodbye, give my regards to Mrs Fenton.

**Fenton**   Oh thanks and mine to Mrs Pratt. Goodbye again, Adamson, and be cautious.

*Exit* **Fenton**.

**Hugh Pratt** (*with hesitation*)   There is something in what Fenton says you know.

**Noah**   There is, but he does not understand the position and I cannot explain it clearly enough for him without making disclosures which I'd rather not make. I prefer to remain silent on matters which I think it unwise to publicly broadcast. Disclosures of that kind of the attitude taken in committee and so on, generally tend to crystallise a man's opposition. I dislike revealing internal dissentions in the Party in face of the class . . .

---

### Scene Three

**Kate Conway**    I'm going to give them my 'Drinking, it's Cause and Cure' at Greens in the morning. What a face Fern has; it's quite Hogarthian. He makes me think of Luther fixing his revolutionary theses on the door of the Church in Wittenberg. What a glorious fight it is. I wonder if the Greek lassies had such times as ours!

**Mrs Hawkins**    Come along now, Miss Conway, and never you mind them Greeks! Miss Martin's that tired she can hardly hold 'er 'ead up and I've got to be up at five to get mine off to 'is work. Come on now we mustn't stop.

**Kate**    Oh I'm coming too, Mrs Hawkins. You always make me think of Palissy, the wonderful potter, throwing the furniture onto the fire for the sake of his great discovery. You're just like Michelangelo's David when you set yourself to . . . [ ].

. . . How you do mother us you dear. You look like one of those beautiful old saints from the windows of Chartres Cathedral.

Oh Noah, be sure to give us one of your sturm and drang speeches at Greens tomorrow; you're to follow me and I shall wait to hear you if Hugh isn't too inexorable . . . [ ] . . . overcome difficulties and you always make me think of Christian Crop crossing Europe with a wheelbarrow. You're like Browning's 'Sordello' –

**Mrs Hawkins** (*seizing* **Kate**'*s arm*)    Oh come Miss Conway, never mind them foreigners . . .

*[ESP notes]: Themes & characters: trade union formation, young suffragettes who take the pledge and their fathers; issues within the movement.*

'. . . come rally etc' (the International).

*Enter* **Noah, Caroline, Martin, Kate, Donovon, Bill Fern, Tom Smith, Hugh Pratt** *and others. Series of speeches from below.* **Noah** *comes to the window.*

**Noah**   No more speeches. It is getting very late and we have a great deal of work to do up here before the morning. Moreover, we've another week before polling day and our voices won't hold out if we use them too recklessly. Remember though that meetings are not all – what really counts is the steady persistent spadework, arguments and systematic distribution of literature. We want more helpers (voters) and everyone who is cheering ought to take up actual work in the movement. And not for the election only, the election is merely an incident. The employing class has far greater resources and means of spreading its propaganda. We can only outdo our opponents in enthusiasm. We appeal to every one of you to come forward. This is your fight as much as ours. Now three cheers for socialism and then goodnight.

**Noah** *leads the cheers, cries of will you come to Weir? Will you come to Pears Yard? Will you come to Boltons?*

**Noah**   Send in a list I'll . . . as far as I can. Goodnight . . .

**Mrs Bullen**   Well I don't mind. I want to speak to whoever's in charge. (*Turning to* **Ruth**.) Are you the young woman that takes the messages?

**Annie**   Yes.

**Mrs Bullen**   Then ask Noah Adamson to come and speak outside Johnson's [Hope Ground] in the dinner hour. About twenty minutes to two would be the best. They're all asking for him. And will he see into the conditions there? I tell you there's women working for fourteen hours a day for six and seven shillings a week! And the dust is something awful. It almost chokes you. And will he see into Musties Turtle Soup company? They say as they make soup for Buckingham Palace! Well *I* wouldn't touch a thing that comes out of there. It makes you fair heave to work in it! And them chickens when we're plucking them they're almost running away from us – they're that high! Thirteen hours a day we work for a matter of ten or eleven shillings a week. There's widows there with big families to bring up. God knows how they manage! I tell you them as eats what's turned out of Musties is as good as eating our flesh and blood! And Mina says if Noah Adamson would come down to the docks any Monday morning he'd see the men fighting for work and hundreds turned away every morning – it's enough to break your heart.

**Ruth Glasier**   I've put it all down and I'll tell him as soon as ever he comes in, but perhaps you'd better give me your name and address.

**Mrs Bullen**   Mrs Bullen. 4 Miller's Place, Perk Street. Noah Adamson's pretty well waked us up down here and we are just going to see whether we can't get things altered.

Don't forget to tell him I'll be round again on Saturday and I'll be able to let you have something then. When I comes near the end of the week I'm all spent up, but I'd like to give a shilling or two to help.

*Enter* **Dick Pyke**, *a pale, very ragged boy about sixteen years of age. He rushes in greatly excited.*

They're all out at Backs! They're coming round in the morning to see Noah Adamson about it. I said I'd slip up and tell you. They'll be here at nine sharp! You've got a bit of waste ground, below, haven't you, where they could hold a meeting?

**Ruth Glasier**   Yes, just round the corner.

**Dick Pyke**   That's all right. Tell Noah Adamson to be ready to speak. They're sure to ask for him and we could do with a few more speakers if you've got any about. I suppose you don't speak yourself? You'd go well with the girls.

**Ruth**   No I don't speak.

**Dick**   Better begin. They came out at five o'clock, couldn't find out where you was at first. That's why they didn't come round tonight but they're all to meet outside the Red Lion in Perk Street tomorrow and I'm to bring them.

*The play moves on to Gasworkers' strike – discussion of wages – of the men and the relative wages of the women –*

They came out at five o'clock, couldn't find out where you was at first. That's why they didn't come round tonight but they're all to meet outside the Red Lion in Perk Street tomorrow and I'm to bring them round. There's five hundred out: the whole shop. Started with the manager giving one of the men the sack and spread all through the place the girls came out as solid as the chaps. These'll be their demands. There may be a few more added, but these'll be the principal. Wages increased all round you see and an hour knocked off every day. They've got married men working in there for eighteen shillings a week and women as low as five. My mother worked there one time for seven shillings, she's a widow you know. D'you think you could drop a line to the Union to send a representative round we could get men joined up easily now they're out.

**Ruth**   Yes, what is it? The Gasworkers?

**Dick**   Yes that'll do. They're mostly labourers. Can you give me a few more of those leaflets I had last time: they seem to go down the best. I could do with any amount. And I'll have another twelve quire of papers. I brought you the money for the last. I had eight quire on Saturday and another four on Tuesday. You'll find it's right. (*Hands her money.*)

**Annie** (*counting*)    You're a good seller! What are you going to sell this week, double?

**Dick**    Oh I don't suppose I can double it, but I might.

**Ruth**    Winnie, reach me down twelve quire of papers. They're counted in quires you know. Get me those leaflets on the green paper. Nellie, a couple of hundred. They're in fifties. (*To* **Dick**.) Yes that's right. Going to take your commission three pence in the shilling on newspapers you know.

**Dick**    Go on put it in the box! What do you take me for!

*Enter* **Mrs Carter**, *stout and ruddy with a large bundle.*

**Mrs Carter**    That's a weight to carry up these stairs – boys' overcoats this time! I do get through some sewing! Good evening Miss Glasier.

**Ruth**    Good evening Mrs Carter.

**Mrs Carter**    I've come to see if Noah Adamson won't do something about old Davis's bug hutches. He put another eighteen pence on them last Monday and it's time he was shown up. Bug hutches that's what they call them and a proper name it is for them, for they're nothing else! The street doors are hanging off the hinges, the stoves are all broken, the chimneys' smoke alarming! There's only one closet to every four houses outside. As for paper and paint – oh well we won't talk about that. You might as well expect a rain of sovereigns as ask for any repairs! And the bugs! It's really a shame that people should live like it. I'm sure when I had to move from Thatcher's Rents through them pulling down to build that great new factory of Green's I never thought I should be living two years in Tiddy's Place! But what can I do? I'm forced to stay there as I was to go there because there isn't another place to be had, so where you look. I've never undone my best bed. It lies bundled up in the cupboard in my front room for fear of getting the bugs

on it and now I'm afraid to open it for fear I shall find the
bugs are on it and that's a fact.

**Nellie**    Oh isn't it a shame! Her best bed!

**Ruth**    It's too bad!

**Mrs Carter**    And now for him to put another 18 pence on!
He only does it because he knows we've nowhere to go.

**Ruth**    Of course!

**Mrs Carter**    It's almost more than flesh and blood can put
up with. When that Salvation Army lass came round on
Tuesday and wanted to pray in my front room I said to her
'you go and pray in old Davies's front room! I reckon he
needs it!' Old Scratty, must be sitting by his bed at night
feeling his pulse to see how soon he'll be able to get his claws
into his fat rat's body. As for his soul I should think Old
Scratty's borrowed that this long time! 'Be off,' I said to her,
'Why should you want to make me into an Angel when I've
got to contend with folk who are worse the poor old Devil
himself. He does have to wait till we are in our coffin!' But I
have to be sharp as a needle after old Davis. He was trying to
make me pay a week twice over less than a month ago. You
tell poor people to be content, I says, well I can't hold with
such opinions. I think poor people should join together and
fight to turn the whole bag of tricks upside down. It's all
wrong at present. You go preaching to those who are
crushing us down! Go to Old Bodger, there's another old
monument of sin. He's like a leech always selling and
hoarding and sending of interest. One of his principal games
is hiring out sewing machines, biding his time, and then
coming down on a woman when she almost paid it all but
just fallen a little in arrears with the last payments – then he
takes the machine and lets it out to some other poor
creature. Oh but he's an Alderman of the Crown and highly
respected! Gives his donations to charity too he says. I've
seen you going into his shop to ask him to be so kind as to
give something in Self Denial week – you never spoke of

praying for his soul did you? And you weren't so truthful as to say he was past praying for either! Oh you are a lot of whited sepulchers! I said to her and so they are! They're always preaching humility to poor folk who are almost too humble to live but they've nothing but compliments for those who are fattening on the backs of the workers although they are puffed up with majestic pride.

It's about time we got the light of socialism, the light of reason I call it, down here. And now we've got one of our own class who has studied and educated himself to be able to fight for us; I think it is due to his workers to come and join him and all the rest of the socialists.

**Dick**    That's what I say and as soon as I heard him speak I said I am with them!

**Mrs Carter**    You're right my lad, but what do you find? You'd be surprised to find poor folk that old Bodger and old Davis and the rest have been screwing the last farthing out of standing up for the rights of property as if they'd been born dukes and duchesses and saying that the whole country will be ruined if the socialists should get in. There's that poor unfortunate Mary Evans! Her man's been in and out of the infirmary ever since the accident. He was in the docks the day after they were married. Twenty-one years since and he never got a penny in compensation, mind you – not a penny. Her eldest lad's in Brixton doing six months on account of the parson calling for the police when the lad and his mates were singing and larking outside the vicarage at eleven o'clock at night. Of course there was a bit of a fight. Her eldest girl is on the streets and she herself is keeping the child the girl had by a master's son when she was in service. That was the beginning of her going wrong; she was only sixteen then. And yet there's that poor woman had the foolish impudence to turn round on me and to say I should be disgraced if my man was to vote for Noah Adamson.

**Peter Jane**    Oh I say that's a good one!

**Mrs Carter**   She said she was told he was an Atheist and against the church and the King.

**Peter Jane**   Good luck to him!

**Mrs Carter**   And she said it was said his mother died in the workhouse.

**Nellie**   But she isn't dead! Well I never!

**Mrs Carter**   I said to her Annie Evans you unfortunate hypocrite where did your mother die? So of course she cries and says you know Mrs Carter I'd never have let her go there if I could have helped it! And I says to her why do you think that poor fellow is any worse than you are?

**Dick**   Oh well I'll have to be off. Good night.

**Miss Glasier**   So long all!

**Annie**   Good night Dick.

**Mrs Carter**   There's my contribution. (*Lays half a crown on the table.*) And I brought you these few flowers my sister's girl fetched over from Woodford wither – she's married that way now. They say it's lovely out there. And here's a few cakes I made perhaps Mrs Adamson might like one. They're only plain.

**Annie**   Thank you very much, you are good.

**Mrs Carter**   I like to do anything I can. Will you give me a few more of those papers to give out? I'll do my best to get them to read them: but it is a job their brains are as dull as those that use the mare sharp and they think they are mighty clever when they are making parrots of themselves – repeating what was in the *Evening News* last night, or what somebody told them was there! I don't know whether Noah Adamson would like to put in one of his articles that at the Mother's Meetings the blankets are all being promised on strict condition that the men don't vote for Adamson. It's for the sake of the country they say. And of course him being against the war tells against him.

**Ruth**   But don't they know that no one can tell how they vote. I thought everyone knew the ballot is secret.

**Mrs Carter**   Supposed to be secret. But they haven't much faith in that – no more have I for that matter. I know there were many got slyly put off their work voting for Adamson last time.

**Ruth**   They must have done more than vote. They must have shown a window card or worn a favour or something.

**Mrs Carter**   Maybe, but many don't think so. I wouldn't put it past them to do anything to keep things their own way. It's true the rich have no call to be frightened yet but if there was a scare that the socialists were going to get in, I'm sure they'd doctor the ballot boxes. I don't see how anyone could think they'd stick at that that has seen how they use the police against the people in a strike and how they'll let it drag on with the children starving. You know, Miss Glasier, I wouldn't say it outside but I'm afraid we're going to be beaten this time.

**Ruth**   Oh don't say that. I don't think so and it's better not to get such an idea into your head.

**Mrs Carter**   It's a very stiff job. First of all he was against the war, you see. And not only have we got the Churches out against us fighting like I've never seen them fight before (and they've always got a finger in the pie), but the publicans that are always busy in the elections are busier than ever. The talk in the bar and a few free drinks has wonderful influence! The publicans are going for Adamson for all their worth because he's a teetotaler as well as being a Socialist: that puts the cup on it! They say 'e's going into Parliament to stop the drink for the working man. 'E couldn't do it last time they say, because of the war but if 'e gets in now it'll be all over that. Goes a long way with a man, the Public House being almost their whole life you might say – outside their work. So we've got the Church and the Public House against us; they always go hand in hand standing up for the rich against all progress. And yet Christ was only a poor man they say and not against the rich by what I can understand of him – reading what he said in the Bible you know seems to me Socialism's the only way to work out what he said people should do, that's my idea of it. But the Parsons are all for the Tories standing up for their own crowd.

**Nellie**  Oh are you sure, Mrs Carter? Don't do to condemn all you know.

**Mrs Carter**  Young woman, you haven't cut your wisdom teeth yet. Do you go to church?

**Nellie**  No.

**Mrs Carter**  No. Your family?

**Nellie**  No.

**Mrs Carter**  Nor to Chapel?

**Nellie**  No.

**Mrs Carter**  Well, you've been spared a lot; but don't you go interrupting when you don't understand. Hold your tongue and learn something. Church is all Tory, Chapel is all Liberal – very few exceptions to that rule and both together for keeping the workers in their place – that means underneath. Well good night, Miss Glasier. Good night all.

**Ruth**  Good night, Mrs Carter, and make up your mind we're going to win.

**Mrs Carter**  Some day, but we've a long road before us and I don't doubt we shall have to do more than voting before socialism comes in. It won't be got so easy as that by a long way. (*Exit* **Mrs Carter**.)

**Peter Jane**  The old girl's right there! There'll be fighting all over the world. Rivers of blood will be shed, both at home and abroad before the capitalists are brought low. We've gone through the Boer War, but that's but a little matter to the wars that lie in front. I wish I could live to see the other

side of it; but it'll take another twenty years to come to a
head I fancy. The workers haven't got an idea yet of the fight
they'll have to make. Even of those who have come to the
idea of socialism, the greater part of them believe they'll get
it by wishing. But the struggle will be very far from that. The
workers will have to come to the point where they'll be
willing, aye, and eager, to risk and to bear more for their
own cause than ever they did for the wars of their masters
– and that's saying much!

Noah Adamson and the rest are doing the work that has to
be done in these days – they are rousing the working class to
know it is exploited and to hate being enslaved; rousing it
from its willingness to sell itself for a weekly wage. We
workers are like a hive of bees working by instinct to make
honey for a scientific beekeeper. We shall have to change our
nature and become like a horde of locusts. I've seen them in
Egypt sweeping down on the country destroying all they
pass over, leaving behind nothing but desolation in their
track. The workers will have to be like that to destroy the
capitalist system. It will seem as though all the good peaceful
workaday nature had gone out of us. We shall be like a pack
of wolves. But after the fighting and terror and tearing
down will come the good new life. The land must be
ploughed before it can be sown. After Noah Adamson and
this generation of pioneers have taught the workers will
come to new leaders who will spur men to act and teach
them to fight. Aye they will fight and be ruthless.

The time will come when lads like young Dick Pyke would be
ashamed to come in with a list of demands like those he
brought here tonight and was so proud. Poor lad he'd made
them up himself, I lay.

The time will come when there'll be no talk of a shilling or
two more on the wages and an hour or so less on the docks
or the machines or in the pits . . . It will be a fight then to put
the workers in possession. Nothing else will be considered.
Lads like Dick will not be talking of speeches on a bit of

waste ground then. They'll be priming their firearms and considering how many guns and how many sturdy marksmen they can muster. Oh yes those days will come, but they'll be twenty years or more to wait for them. Who can say what country it will start with. Like enough where it's least expected. But come it will.

**Ruth**   Now Mr Jane don't get downhearted.

**Peter Jane**   Downhearted my girl! Don't you imagine that. My mind's like a great bird with strong wings soaring up to the sun when I think of it! If only I could be your age to have the same hope of fighting beside them! I tell you there'll be young women like you in those days that will shoulder the rifle and march off with the lads to fight as brave and proud as any of them.

Aye, those'll be great days. And after the fighting then will come the sunshine! Then you'll see the youngsters growing up like flowers of a morning! Those'll be the good days! Then folk will turn to each other in friendliness and share their unstinted plenty. All these dark streets will gone. There'll be flashing white marble and colours as bright as any I saw in Egypt. The flowers in front of the houses will smell so sweet you'd fancy yourself in Covent Garden shops! You'll have better things to do than look in shops. Young maidens gaping in, as you do, you hussies, at all the best you can't afford to buy. There won't be shops as we know them today, in those times – places where people sit like spiders in a web waiting till someone comes in, but you'll be able to get all the clothes you want.

---

*Now sections that are copies and inconsecutive pages – there are up to 5/6/7 numbers of repeated p. 20s, 21s, 22s. Below is my piecing together from all of them.*

# Act III

## Scene One

*After twenty-five years.*

**Noah**'s *room in London. An old-fashioned place with walls painted dark green. The fireplace. A hob. On each side engravings of William Morris, Karl Marx, Robert Owen, Ernest Jones and others. Engravings of incidents of the Chartist struggle, etc. A few paintings on the wall opposite the fireplace which is least used and set very high so as to be little seen. A window seat. A chair on the floor. A round table in the centre of the room. Armchairs, one either side the fire and two very small round tables, one of which is [illegible] and the other beside one of the armchairs. [Note: This description of set is facsimile of photographs of Keir Hardie's lodgings at Nevill's Court.]*

**Noah**, **Thomas Fenton** *and* **Hugh Pratt** *are together.* **Thomas Fenton** *is [follow-on page missing].*

*Enter* **Freda McLaird**, *about twenty-five years . . . [line crossed out but then next lines do follow]*

**Noah**    Is it to be tea or coffee?

**Freda**    I'd better say which ever you've got, hadn't I?

**Noah**    I'm afraid you had. The coffee is all finished.

**Freda**    Then I choose tea.

**Noah**    Thank you, you are very kind.

**Freda**    Do you remember the first time we had coffee?

**Noah**    Don't be a tease.

---

**Freda**    Very well I shall talk seriously. Mrs Sedgfield was here just before I came.

**Noah**    Yes. How did you know?

**Freda**    Because I was on my way here and she told me she was going to see you as . . .

---

**Noah**    Did you read the article?

**Freda**    Yes.

**Noah**    What was wrong with it?

**Freda**    Oh not much it is most interesting.

**Noah**    I wasn't satisfied with it. I told you I went through it twice, dictating of course. I've been too busy, no spare time to write it.

**Freda**    Well, I think it is because you were tired the first time you dictated it that the arrangement wasn't very good. I went through it and rearranged the sections, leaving the old numbers on the pages so you could go back to them if you preferred. By my arrangement you can discard several pages that are repetition, and you would have to rewrite a few. I put slips of paper with notes on to show you what I mean. I can't see anything else wrong with the article. I think it is excellent.I hope you won't mind my suggestions – you told me to do it you know. Here it is.

**Noah**    Mind! No of course not! Thank you so much, Freda. Aren't you going to have milk in your tea?

**Freda**    I'm trying it without I think I like it better. And you were so much astonished not long ago when you found I took coffee without milk that evening in the restaurant in Sloane Square after we'd been to the Court Theatre.

**Noah**    I was I admit I was as much astonished as if you'd called for a cigar.

**Freda**    Why?

**Noah**    Well . . . I was.

**Freda**   Do you remember that day I fainted.

**Noah**   I do indeed!

**Freda**   You looked so terribly upset! Well do you know I should have liked to ask for some brandy, but I was afraid you'd be shocked.

**Noah**   Not at all.

**Freda**   But you didn't offer me any.

**Noah**   I never thought of it.

**Freda**   I believe you would have been shocked; it's only about two or three years since you thought the theatre a wicked place, isn't it?

**Noah**   Oh you'll have to add a nought to that.

**Freda**   Twenty or thirty years ago! Oh it isn't nearly as long as that, you know it isn't.

---

*Page 8 missing*

*Page 9 continues:*

. . . though she guessed I was and didn't want me to come with her.

**Noah**   So what did you do?

**Freda**   I went and sat on Oliver Goldmith's grave stone by the Round Church in the Temple.

**Noah**   Weren't you afraid of spooks?

**Freda**   Good gracious no. I like Oliver Goldsmith. [*ESP struck through the following lines:*] ~~I read a story about him once that made him seem a bit like you. I don't suppose he was really.~~ I shouldn't mind seeing his spook at all. Mrs Sedgfield was very angry.

**Noah**  Yes, witch! How did you know that?

**Freda**  Because I've read the evening papers and know what Bills the Labour Party is introducing and that it won't make any amendments to the address.

**Noah**  Yes, she was angry.

**Freda**  She said you'd gone back on your speech at the conference.

**Noah**  Yes, she said that.

**Freda**  She didn't understand that you meant you'd leave the Party if your freedom to support Votes for Women were interfered with, not that you would leave the Party if the Party as a Party wouldn't make itself responsible for anything short of Adult Suffrage. ~~That was what you meant wasn't it, you meant you'd leave the. . .~~

~~NOAH:~~

~~That's it the firstiswhat I meant~~

**Freda**  The first is what you meant and the second is what she thought you ought to mean. Isn't that it?

**Noah**  Yes that's it exactly.

**Freda**  Did you explain to her?

**Noah**  Not very well. I'm not good at defending myself.

**Noah** *takes galley proof from the table, marks a passage in pencil and passes it over to* **Freda**.

That's my article for this week.

**Freda**  Did you show it to Mrs Sedgfield?

**Noah**  No.

**Freda**  You'll get into trouble with the Labour Party for saying if you had a place in the ballot you would have given it to Votes for Women whatever the Party might have said – and I'm afraid you won't get much thanks from the WSPU

– not from their women or their circle. You see, they think
you ought to be able to make the Labour Party do
everything you want. They can't really bring themselves to
believe you can't. They think it is like the Prime Minister and
the Cabinet responsibility – you being the Prime Minister
and the Cabinet the Labour Members of Parliament. They
make you responsible for the whole thing and refuse to
conceive of you being outvoted and forced to submit to
decisions you hate.

**Noah**    That's it: it is one of the penalties of Party Office.

**Freda**    But ~~everyone outside the WSPU or most people~~ in
the Labour Party they consider you've ~~gone~~ (you're) quite
mad on the subject of Votes for Women and make you
responsible for all our sins.

**Noah**    Yes.

**Freda**    You're between two fires.

**Noah**    They're very warm sometimes.

**Freda**    Mrs Sedgefield doesn't see, most of our women
don't see, that it isn't only a question of the Labour Party
being unsatisfactorily lukewarm at the best on the subject of
Votes for Women only; but on every question. They don't
realize that if you were making up your mind to take the
serious step – they don't realize it's serious – of leaving the
Labour Party – it would be on the fundamental question of
the Class struggle. They don't realize it's breaking your heart
about that as anyone can see. Mrs Sedgfield would realize if
she'd let herself think – but most of them have no conception
of such things – If one hadn't any other reason for guessing
it, it was plain enough when you made that speech at the
Labour Party dinner in the House of Commons Party dinner
about the Anti-Guzzling League you were going to form.
They didn't like it when you said that the Liberals and Tories
only offered their hospitality to Labour for that . . . for a
world . . . Members to break down their hostility and gain an
influence over them. They hate it when you said we're only

guys for them. They don't think they are and they're proud of being made friends of the Liberals and Tories.

**Noah**   It's a byword. [*Missing page.*] . . . That Mackintosh is always on the doorstep of Cabinet Ministers – I don't want to speak of it Freda.

**Freda**   You never do. It's I who do all the talking.

**Noah**   Come, think of something else. ~~Sit by the fire whilst I clear the cups.~~

**Freda**   Let me do it.

**Noah**   No.

**Freda**   Well I must help.

**Noah**   No, sit.

*He takes away the little table and takes the other armchair.*

**Noah**   What book have you there?

**Freda** (*takes up a volume she has placed on the arm of the chair*) Romanian Folk Songs! They are extraordinary. I think if you were to give them to children brought up far away from the world they would know all the essential things about life. They are nearly all sad, but that's true too isn't it. Each one has a little refrain that seems to have no relation to the song and yet it has. I read them every night now, I'm always thinking of them. Some of them are terrible. I think the song: I looked up on the saint and fear came on me / The willows shivered for they hid the sun –

I think this is charming –

Yea the night knows my song for she has told it to the stars in Heaven.

The Little stars / Little . . . [*rubbed off, illegible*]

. . . to whom it seems so sweet that every evening they return and listen to hear my song from me.

Another says: Look not upon this sky at eventide for that makes sorrowful the heart of man.

Look rather here into my heart and joyful shalt thou then always be. –

Isn't that like you feel in the evening outside in the country on a quite calm evening when the sun sets in a clear sky, don't you feel a sadness almost unbearable overwhelming. Read one to me . . .

[. . .]

**Noah**   I never could speak of what I felt most deeply. I have always had to suffer without words.

**Freda**   Oh I don't believe it – you only imagine so because you're so lonely here by yourself that you forget I'm only a little girl, but your girl, that you get these fancies. I never thought I couldn't imagine you thought of me as anything else than the daughter of two old friends; your little girl who had not her own father. How could I think of —

/ love and then shoved it back in the back without seeing that it wanted a little affection . . .

**Noah**   Yes.

Do you remember the little pussy you told me about . . . the one the man on the bus was carrying?

I . . . letting pussy . . . on the bus.

**Freda**   When the man examined it and its . . .

I'm in such a hurry. But I don't know why I'm telling you all this. It's only sometimes I feel like that life is precarious at present isn't it. And I do waste time don't I when I come talking nonsense to you.

**Noah**   Not nonsense.

**Freda**   But I'm not a little pussy.

**Noah**   No you are not a little pussy.

**Noah** *leaves his chair crosses over and sits on the arm of* **Freda**'s.
~~Freda moves to lean forward to avoid touching him then gradually~~
~~? her cheek nervously with her hand then her face clears ? and gently~~
~~around him~~

*He touches her cheek with his hand.*

**Freda** *starts slightly and leans forward to avoid touching him.*

**Noah**    Have you never wanted to feel a man's arms around
you in love? The [*illeg*] arms.

**Freda** [*illeg*] *slowly with a sigh and gently puts her closed hand
against his cheek to hold him back looks at him sadly then with a low*
. . .

Oh you have other people . . .

**Noah**    I'll give up the other people.

**Freda** (*proudly*)    I shouldn't like you to do that I shouldn't
like to be the cause of making anyone else unhappy.

**Noah**    You know I am too fond of you Freda.

**Freda**    What does it mean?

**Noah**    Just what it says.

**Freda** (*drops her head*)    Oh let me be still your little girl
always and not spoil the little flower.

*He withdraws his hand and sits quite still.* **Freda** [*illeg*] *and
gradually leans so that she just touches him.*

*After some moments he slips onto his knees and puts his arms round
her gently.*

**Noah**    Are you longing sometimes.

**Freda** *bolts upright and looks at him.*

**Noah**    You had better go, then you'll be quite safe. Better
take care of yourself.

**Freda** *looks at him miserably. He helps her to put on her coat? Then opens the door and motions to her to precede him.*

**Noah**    I'll come down with you.

---

*Unnumbered:*

**Freda**    I can't judge you I don't understand only I can see this. We must not make anyone else unhappy. ~~I must not injure your work and if I thought I was going to bring a child into the world that didn't get a fair chance I'd kill myself~~

**Noah**    It is to be all sacrifice?

**Freda**    Can't you forget that we ever talked like this and be as before . . .

**Noah**    Freda only a minute ago I was so happy. I didn't realize it but I was happier . . .

*Unnumbered:*

I don't know. I don't understand. I thought of it . . . if it had been my father and my mother . . . should . . . I can't judge you without I should think of it was anyone else I can't think anything but good of you I . . .

*Unnumbered:*

. . . you politically. It would be brought up at your election and brought up in the Party. I wouldn't do anything to inure you and would injure the movement by injuring you . . .

*Unnumbered:*

. . . anything else I [?] couldn't? believe it. Tell me it isn't true.

**Noah**    Wouldn't you like to have a little baby?

**Freda**    What . . . about? A baby . . . I . . . with it . . .

**Noah**    I would love it.

**Freda** (*between laughter and tears*)    Oh poor little creature how would I rear it? I find it so hard to live . . . if I seriously thought there was a possibility of Mrs Sedgfield agreeing to anything like that . . . that would put another burden on you, that would make your hard road harder. Don't you realize that anything of that kind . . . anything so much as that . . . any talk about you and me . . . would be used against . . .

---

**Fragment:**

**Noah**    Oh you need not trouble about privacy, you can speak before my Comrades.

**Peter Jane**    As I'm in the road I'll be off.

**Noah**    No, Comrade, don't go. I don't have anything private to say to these gentlemen.

What is the business you have come on?

**Lyle**    I want to discuss a little matter with you, Mr Adamson – that I feel sure will interest you, but as the matter is confidential I should prefer to see you alone.

---

**Fragment:**

. . . come and speak to them and she hears the same is true on the men's side and in the body of the House.

**Ruth**    I'm sure Mr Adamson would be glad to do it, but I don't know if the Board could be got to allow it.

However I'no everything will be tried.

**Old Woman**    Indeed it's a pleasure to hear him and a wonderful comfort. Every word he says is as true as Gospel. I only wish I could live to see it. Thanking you kindly, Mrs, for putting my words before him. It would give me heart in there if you could manage it. I brought him these two new laid eggs for his breakfast. They were only laid this morning so I know they're fresh.

**Annie**   Thank you it's very kind of you.

**Old Woman**   If you'll be so kind as to put it before him; good night miss.

**Annie**   Good night.

*Enter* **Mrs Bullen** *and young married woman about thirty,* **Nellie**.

How d'you . . .

**Mrs Bullen**   I am surprised to see you, are you coming along to join the . . .

---

**Fragment:**

**Lyle**   No one was prepared for it. You certainly did very well, it's a tribute to your eloquence, but of course you know that if there'd been any serious effort made to oppose you you couldn't possibly have got in. A man of your perception must realize that. May I take it you agree?

**Noah**   Do you want a statement from me that I don't expect to win the election?

**Lyle**   Oh, Mr Adamson, you don't suppose I'd have come here on such an errand! Indeed no. This is quite a confidential business.

---

**Fragment:**

**Noah**   Good night all.

**Adamson**  Thank you.

**Winnie**  Good night.

**Bill Fermer**  Well I'll be going, Noah.

**Tom Smith**  I think I shall have to be moving too – *general handshake and good nights exeuent all except* **Noah**, **Hugh Pratt** *and* **Peter Jane**.

*Knock.*

*Pratt opens.*

*Enter Mesrs* **Barker**, **Dickson** *and* **Lyle**.

**Barker** *is a fat short red-faced man with a heavy gold watch chain.*

**Barker**  I've brought some gentlemen to see you that are desirous of meeting you. I'm sure you'll be very pleased to meet'em. This is Mr Adamson, Mr Lyle – Let me 'ave the pleasure Mr Lilie, Mr Dickson, Mr Adamson.

**Noah**  What can I do for you?

**Dickson** *is a tall pale man in a frock coat and silk hat rather pale and bored looking.* **Lyle** *is of medium height with light-grey silk spats and a white waistcoat with a dark black beard, white teeth and a rather bland appearance.*

**Barker**  May we come in, Mr Adamson?

---

**Mr Barker**  These gentlemen wanted to 'ave the pleasure of meetin' you Mr Adamson to 'ave a little talk with you I believe and I made so bold as to volunteer to introduce 'em feelin' sure as you'll be pleased for to make their acquaintance.

**Peter Jane**  I don't think Noah Adamson knows who you are, George Barker.

**Noah**  No I don't know him.

**Hugh**   I seem to have seen you at our meetings: if I'm not mistaken your –

**Barker**   Oh I don't agree with all you –

---

**Fragment:**

**Lyle**   I am speaking to you as a man of the world: it's impossible for you to win.

**Noah**   Suppose that were the case it wouldn't make any difference to my contesting the seat.

**Lyle**   Obviously not, Mr Adamson, since you are contesting it, Mr Adamson, but let us talk seriously. Under present conditions you cannot win the seat; but you might under other circumstances – with other support – Other and stronger influences to back you. You take me?

**Noah**   I hear what you say.

**Adamson**   Such support . . .

**Lyle**   The matter is strictly confidential and I take it that this gentleman, your friend, will fully understand. The fact is, Mr Adamson, you can't win this election you know. You must be aware of it. You got in last time by a fluke you know, because –

**Peter Jane**   I'll have to be off any road, Noah. My missus'll be wondering what's become of me as it is so long see you on't morning.

**Hugh**   If I'm in the way. . .

**Noah**   Certainly not. (*To* **Lyle**.) I must ask you to be brief. I am busy . . .

---

**Lyle**   . . . and so on the usual respect to the Party of course – a man doesn't lose his personal independence of course –

it's a question of *savoir vivre* you know – purely that – and now I come to the more solid and palatable part of the business and these would be £300 a year for yourself during the Parliament whether you were elected or not and a safe seat for you at the general election.

~~NOAH.~~

~~You deserve a thrashing but~~

**Noah**   You've come on a fool's errand and you're wasting my time. Show them out Hugh and see that the door is fastened.

**Lyle**   Good night, Mr Adamson.

*Exeuent all but* **Noah** *who writes.*

**Hugh** (*opens the door*)   I'm afraid you'll find the stairs rather dark.

**Fragment:**

**Lyle**   . . . possible to give the necessary backing you should call yourself a Liberal Labour candidate, of course you would wish to retain the title Labour in all its prominence and on being elected you would receive the Liberal whips and so might be – would be forthcoming under certain conditions if the support were suitably received if certain reasonable guarantees were given: in short the proposal is that in order to make it . . .

---

*Unnumbered:*

**Lyle**   We've known him down these parts for a good few years Noah – ever since we started almost.

**Mr Barker**   Well I'll be going, gentlemen. I've done my part, no offence meant, Mr Adamson. Good night to you, Noah. (*To* **Lyle** *and* **Dickson**) What . . . say far from . . . I don't hold with *all* Mr Adamson's ideas.

**Peter Jane**   And you come kickin' up a row at our meetings with your gang – them as you pay to do it, or as I should say them as is paid by them as pays . . . to organize it.

**Scene Three**

**Noah** *shuts window.*

**Bill Fermer**   I would have given them a few words.

**Kate Conway**   Or I –

**Noah**   No more tonight. You're hoarse already Katherine.

**Kate**   I've had eight glorious meetings – I have them tonight – my 'Cry of the Children' at –

---

**Noah**   Maynard said he didn't know which to admire most, the woman who made the speech or the audience that so received it. Hugh will give you a list of pitches for tomorrow I'm afraid he's asking for you in the breakfast hour.

**Kate** (*to* **Hugh**)   Oh, I have you got the proofs of the posters for the town hall meetings yet?

**Hugh**   No.

**Kate**   Be sure to see that he puts in my bit – you know I always insist on using it – though the University doesn't allow it. Let them prosecute me!

**Mrs Hawkins**   Will you take a cup of tea, Miss Conway?

**Kate**   Thank you dear, call me Kate. How you do mother us! (*To* **Bill**.) Your speaking has done wonders informed comrade you did famously tonight.

. . .

Just so tired (*to* **Hugh**) Have you got a canvassable book for me?

**Hugh**   Aren't you afraid of over doing it? I've got you down for a lot of meetings you know.

**Caroline**   I shall if lose my voice when it's over.

**Mrs Harkins** (*to* **Caroline**)   I should go home lass if I was you, you look played out. I'm going your way, come along with me now. You too, Miss Conway, come along home now or you'll never be at those breakfast meetings.

**Caroline**   Oh Kate is never late.

*Exit* **Kate, Caroline, Mrs Hawkins**

**Noah** (*to* **Winnie**)   You and Jack will be going home now won't you?

**Winnie**   Is it late?

**Noah**   I'm afraid your mother will think so. Also, I want you to do something for me. If you go at one you'll just catch Mr Williams before he leaves. He's working 'til 11.00. I want you to take him this packet and say we want the leaflets as soon as ever he can print them.

**Winnie**   I'll go as quick as I can, but when shall I tell Mother you'll be in?

**Noah**   Tell her I've got the key and not to wait up. I'll make myself a cup of tea if I want it.

**Winnie**   All right, Noah. (*To* **Jack**.) Come along, Jack. Good night all.

---

**Kate**   Your simile about horses and men reminded me of a passage in Shakespeare's *Henry VII*?

**Caroline**   Shakespeare didn't write a Henry VII.

**Kate**   Oh yes he did.

**Caroline**   He didn't.

**Kate**   Oh no I can't allow you to say that, Caroline, I know he did I know because I wrote my thesis for my BA.

**Caroline**   Refresh your memory when you get home.

**Mrs Hawkins** (*to* **Caroline**)   Here lass take a cup of tea, you look fair done.

**Caroline**   Thank you. I expect . . .


**Scene Four**

**Noah**   Don't be too confident. The meetings are good but you aren't doing enough of the spadework.

**Tom Smith**   Oh the canvass don't count. I don't believe in it myself, nothing like a good rousing meeting.

**Noah**   We only get a certain minority of the electorate at the meetings and as we have no press to enable us, we can only approach the majority through canvassing and leaflets.

---

**Hugh Pratt** *takes a pile of little books and begins sorting them into piles . . .*

---

**Noah**   Remember too that it isn't the meetings alone that count. The steady and persistent work, the grind of arguments and distribution of literature by those who don't speak is still more important. We want volunteers for every kind of work. We want you all to help and not for the elections only. This is one election . . . This is only an incident in the struggle. Now three cheers for Socialism and good night.

**Noah** *leads the cheers then shuts the window.*

**Bill Fern**   Grand meeting Noah.

**Noah**, *now alone on stage.*

**Noah**    Freda? . . . Oh . . . used . . . you . . . looked like a man in the gloom/dim [?] . . . fine . . . in . . . suffering? Suffrage? And . . . Yourself . . . after . . . believed . . . now I spent here . . . in all . . . our like? Life? Is it . . . reveal your . . . make yourself . . . hard and cold but here with me your eye always . . . to me . . . but . . . like . . . sunshine . . .